The Children's Story

The Children's Story

© 2016 by Al and Susan Miner

Cover art and book design by Susan M. Miner

Library of Congress number: 2016942610
ISBN: 9781941915080

1. Lama Sing 2. Psychics 3. Trance Channels 4. Life After Death
I. Miner, Al II. Lama Sing III. Title

Printed in the United States of America

Note: What follows is a summary of 20 readings that were combined into a book titled *When Comes the Call,* a body of work considered by many to be the most foundational and contributive of over 10,000 readings given by Al Miner and Lama Sing.

It is the story of the history of the Children of God, including the birth and "entrapment" of humanity, and the imminent coming Promise of the return of *utter* Free Will Choice. Free will choice is a term often bantered about and believed to varying degrees, though most would not believe theirs is the choice over pestilence, disease, geographic or societal conditions, and death itself. Yet this and more is The Promise: the original truth of absolute and total freedom of what one experiences. In order to more fully understand this promise, one needs to understand what happened to the original state of Freedom.

The book *When Come the Call* has been summarized because some found it difficult to follow. Perhaps this little summary will whet your appetite for the detail that can be found in the book. At the least, it offers a brief history of our lineage from the Beginning.

~~~~~~

Imagine that you are Consciousness.

You have only this one awareness ...
that you are at peace
and that you are.

~~~~~~

Within the loving Darkness the Children of God are born, emerging in the awareness of themselves, of one another, and of the utter preciousness of each as a Divine expression of God. They rejoice and celebrate their discovery of themselves and of each other, and then become aware that something lies beyond. God gives them all the greatest gift after life itself - Free Will.

Some choose, then, to set out to explore the movement of the living Darkness into the Light: the Expression of God.

Others choose to remain Home in the Darkness: the Embrace of God.

Those who choose to remain Home *know* the essences, the Color, of God as God expands; those who choose to explore *experience* the Color.

In that which lies beyond Home is the Nothingness and the All, the Sacred Silence and the Word going forth, the breath and the expression of God. At the "far edge" is the billowing, rolling Color of God – pure potential – ever and ever expanding.

Throughout the All, as at Home, the knowing of the Children of God to be precious expressions of God is also ever expanding.

Those Children who have moved out to experience the expression of God soon discover how to shape the very Color of God. Among these who choose to experience is One who chooses to remain in the embrace *simultaneously!* Meaning that, no matter how far out this One explores, He has chosen to do so ever in the complete Consciousness and experience of the Presence of God. So brilliant is He in the ease of His steadfastness, in His peaceful oneness with God, that the Light of His own presence wherever he goes is as brilliant as the very Light of God. He comes to be known as the Shining One. There are Brethren who journey with Him who are, likewise, as dedicated to ever being present with God.

The Children move further and further out into expression, each time returning joyfully to tell God and their brethren of their experiences.

A few of the Children who are learning to create with essences of God, so enjoying the wonder of their experiences, have the thought to return a gift to God of their own making, a sort of mirror image in miniature of God's own unfolding creation.

These brothers and sisters decide that, while they carry on with creating their gift, they will sequester themselves away from the knowing of God and all others, an impossibility but they do so anyway within the gift of the Universal Law of Free Will. Though they believe (and thus it this so *for them*, these certain brothers and sisters) that they are building their creation in secret, all others know separation is impossible, and so this place where some of the brothers and sisters are creating comes to be known as the place-that-cannot-be, or the No-Place.

The intention to be sequestered wraps, veil-like, veil

after veil and inter-between after inter-between, all about the brothers and sisters, sequestering them (only because they *believe* it to be so) from all that lies beyond.

It comes to be known among all the other Children that the brothers and sisters who have gone off to "be alone" in their creative works are moving so deep into the allure of being creators that they are forgetting more and more the true Source of all creation. They are coming to believe that their tiny mirror image, albeit also ever expanding, is all there is.

Some of the Children become curious about what is being created and go to find their brothers and sisters. This intent is led by Yo-El. The Light of Yo-El's intent creates a sort of pathway before him for him and others joining him to follow.

Nearly immediately, they are stopped in their journey by the veils that are binding those within the No-Place in their intent to be alone in their creation.

Coming up against this stuns Yo-El and the others, for they have never experienced anything before that intends separateness. So, Yo-El and the others leave to ask God about this upsetting curiosity.

God tells them that it is not as Yo-El and the others believe… not that these brothers and sisters are actually intending to be separate, only that they do not wish to be disturbed in their creating:

"It is wondrous, is it not. They have constructed their world in such a way that they can be a part of my creative energy while, seemingly, apart from it," God tells them.

He then tells them,

"As you come upon something unknown to you, remember me and I will know it with you and, together, we shall always find gladness in our journeys. And always remember, too… You have my gift of Choice. If you find that something does not gladden you within, deny it not nor judge it. Simply decide your joy is elsewhere and be about that joy."

Some who are present do as God has said… They consider their choices and, deciding that their joy is not with the creating taking place in the No-Place, leave the group.

Those who are left, for the first time, have a feeling, a missing.-thing.

Knowing this, God tells them to remember that all are,

ever, one. Then God leaves the Children to the experience of their own choosing.

The Children consider what God has just given, that there is only Oneness, and they consider their brothers and sisters deep in their experience of separateness.

Out of deep love for them, the Children construct the memory of Oneness around them in order that, should these brothers and sisters ever wish it, the gift of Oneness is only a choice away.

God knows of their loving intent, their construction, and sends them His laughter:

"Ah, Children, your loving intention to embrace your brothers and sisters in the knowing that we are ever one has inadvertently created another impossibility, a structure similar to their veils around this Place-That-Cannot-Be."

The Children laugh at what they have done, and then turn to see the beauty of their intent in form. They decide to call their gift the Heaven-Place.

After this, greater awareness and honor that they should not violate in any way the choices of their brothers and sisters in the No-Place, Yo-El leads the Children who have remained with him back to observe the creation that is taking place.

They move through veil after veil and interbetween after interbetween before coming to a loosely forming structure that is coming to be known as the Earth-Place. Yo-El notes that the creations have not been given freedom as have all of God's creations elsewhere, and it seems to him, therefore, that God must be absent. He and the others call out, asking God about this.

God summons Yo-El and the Children from throughout all of Consciousness, any who are willing, Home. Even some from deep within the No-Place feel the loving summons and instantly return Home.

Touching all present with the Light of His love, God places a gift within each, a proclamation:

"I am ever with you. This shall, and ever shall, be."

He then instructs them all to find joy in one another's choices. They dance about one another in full comprehension and celebration of this wondrous gift.

Yo-El recognizes one from the Earth-Place to be a brother known as Il-Em. Yo-El goes to him and, Il-Em, recognizing Yo-El, rushes to him and their energies become one.

Then, Il-Em invites Yo-El and the Children with him

back to the Earth-Place to see what they are now creating. All agree and Il-Em excitedly leads them to where they can observe from within the veil just beyond the Earth-Place.

While Il-Em is excited and proud of the accomplishments, Yo-El and the others are stunned. The brothers and sisters in the Earth-Place have fashioned forms around the Light of their spirit given to them by God! To the forms, they have attached appendages with which they reach out to take of the essences of God to create other various forms. Some have somehow managed to entreat another to climb into their creations. The ones inside these creations appear unable to escape, while the creators do not seem to notice. Newly arriving brothers and sisters are learning and joining in with these ways.

Yo-El and the Children honor Il-Em and his joy as best they can, as God has taught them, and they tell him they'll leave them to their creations. Il-Em happily returns to his creating as Yo-El and the others rush away.

They are met in the beyond by the Shining One and His Brethren. He reminds Yo-El and the others of their intent of love when they created the Heaven-Place. Then he calls their attention to another creation.

Near the Heaven-Place is a beautiful thoughtform. All

throughout this thoughtform, this "place", are brethren who are also creating with the essences of God, but here the creations remain free and the Light of their own spirit has not been covered over.

The Children are in wonder as they hear God explain:

"What you bring to a thing is what it becomes for you. It forms as you believe it to be. This is always so. It is you who allow it, or nay.

"This realm is pure. These brothers and sisters moved here from the No-Place when they saw what was happening to the original intent of goodness there. They do not judge. They have merely chosen to create here in peace, ever honoring the freedom I have intended for all creation. And ever in their experiencing here they are aware that they can be with me whenever they choose. Some have returned and remain with me. Others move to and fro."

The Shining One tells them, "While these brethren here play in and with the gifts of God in imitation and in discovery as do their brothers and sisters in the No-Place, they do so in Oneness, not in the illusion of separateness.

"I and my Brethren often come here, for when a great call is issued from within the No-Place, these brothers and sisters will join with many others who will move into the

No-Place to open the way for those who have forgotten.

The Shining One invites the Children to return with Him to the Earth-Place, where they see that, just since they've been away, much has transpired.

Yo-El is struck that the Light of the spirit of these brothers and sisters is now completely hidden. Few now can recognize or remember the Light of Spirit in another.

The Shining One knows the sorrow of Yo-El and the Children. "Though they have, indeed, forgotten, theirs is nonetheless a love seeking to better know itself. This feeling you have – that God is not – is an illusion. It was created in and sustained throughout the Earth-Place because they wish to understand, to truly know, what it is to be one with God by experiencing being apart from Him. As they search and seek to remember, give them your love."

Yo-El and the Children leave and move off into the All to simply *be* in the Peace of God.

After awhile, one of great golden brilliance comes to them. He is the Guardian of the Way. He urges them to pause in their *be*-ing to listen.

Yo-El hears something, feels something, that tugs at him. When he asks about this, the Guardian simply tells

Yo-El to know it for himself, that he only came to bring the choice to Yo-El's attention.

Yo-El and the Children follow that which tugs at them, and find themselves at the edge of the Heaven-Place. They are met by some of the Shining One's Brethren. These Brethren are still shining in their essence but they have taken on form similar to the brothers and sisters in the Earth-Place. Yo-El asks about this and they explain that this is so that, when the brothers and sisters begin to depart the Earth-Place and come to the Heaven-Place for rest, that the presence of the Brethren will be more or less familiar and will not alarm them.

Yo-El asks about what he is hearing that is calling to him. The Brethren explain that there are some who are wanting to leave the No-Place but they have lost their way. Yo-El asks how this is possible, since it was their free choice to be there and, if they choose to leave it, why they don't simply do so.

The Shining One appears and explains. "They have built a belief of separation so powerful that they now know only this. It is a no-thing but they believe it to be a thing, and thus it is. They no longer remember that they are free. Deep within, they remember something. It urges them so much that they wish to know what it is, to go to it, but because they do not remember how to find their way out of the illusion, they call."

Yo-El asks how he and his brethren can help and is told that this can't be given to him, that he would need to experience it for himself, so they go back into the No-Place towards the Earth-Place.

Along the way they come upon some brothers and sisters in one of the veils who are calling out while haphazardly zigzagging all about. Yo-El goes up to one of the callers to ask what he is doing but the caller doesn't hear, so Yo-El shines the Light of his loving intent to the caller. This stirs the caller into a pause of sorts, which, in turn, stirs the others who had been chaotically moving all about, calling. Immediately, Yo-El and the Children gather up all the callers and rush them out of the No-Place.

Once they are settled and the Light of their spirit is returning, Yo-El recognizes a caller and goes up to him.

The caller searches the one before him and asks softly, "Is it you, my brother?"

Yo-El answers. "Yes, Il-Em, it is I."

Their Lights become as one, and then the Children gather around the callers as Il-Em tells of many things that have been transpiring in the Earth-Place. He shares how, at first, his brothers and sisters intended simply to celebrate God with each new creation. But then, they began to want their creations to the very best, and so they compared and competed for recognition until they actually began destroying each other's creations.

When Il-Em is finished recounting, his essence begins to do a weeping-thing. Suddenly, God is in their midst.

Il-Em rushes to God, and God embraces him and tells him that He was always there with Il-Em. It was only Il-Em's choice to make the distance seem real:

> *"But you remembered and called out, and now the illusion is no more and we are as we were in the beginning."*

Il-Em's weeping-thing begins to subside and Yo-El goes to him. "You remembered God?"

Il-Em answers, "Deep within, I remembered something, but we had to use care, for those who did not wish us to believe in that which was beyond the Earth-Place would gather upon us with such force that we could not muster sufficient to resist… and so… we became as theirs."

Yo-El and the others are stunned.

A group who had been with Yo-El rushes away, calling back, "They cannot do this! This is not righteous.

We will rescue those who are being dominated."

The others remaining call after them but it is too late. The rescuers are gone.

The Children start to do the missing and weeping-things, but Il-Em warns them, "Do not give it life. If you give it life, if you give it your sorrow, I tell you, it grows with swiftness until it seems to take on a beingness of its own, and before you are aware of it, you come to know that it is within you! So you desperately try to bring it out, realizing that you *allowed* it into you, but the more you try, the more you also realize that it has gained such a power that you finally give up trying to rid yourself of it."

Again, the Children are stunned. They move into their Light within to balance with what they have just been given.

When they have returned the Peace of God to themselves, Yo-El and Il-Em speak with them of how they might safely retrieve the rescuers, knowing the rescuers have placed themselves in grave danger in order to save the brothers and sisters who have, seemingly, lost the power of their will.

The Shining One appears now and shows them how to use an energy intent to move instantly in and out and all about the No-Place without disturbing, without violating, the right of free will choice of those within. So Yo-El, Il-Em, and these Children move, within the energy Intent, to the Earth-Place to find the rescuers.

There, they discover how the combined thought of those brothers and sisters who intend to dominate, to control, has taken on another kind of energy. This energy, hovering about, luring, influencing the brothers and sisters into its fold, is known in Consciousness as the massmind-thing.

From within the energy Intent, moving about the Earth-Place without disturbing their choices, the Children hear a weak call. They follow it finally locate the rescuers.

The rescuers are all inside a sort of residence. They have resisted the influence of the massmind-thing, and here, within this dwelling, they are doing all they know to do to not be discovered by those who would intend them harm, for the insidious massmind-thing guides the discovery and influences the destruction of the intent for freedom from it by any who who begin to remember.

Yo-El knows he must go to the rescuers. He and Il-Em and another leave the Intent, They cover their Light with stuff of the earth, taking on the forms of the brothers and sisters, and go to the rescuers. Those remaining in the Intent extend their own intention of safety, their Light, disguising it as best they can, to this rescue. The three make it inside the dwelling but not without suspicion by a growing group that is beginning to gather around the residence.

Inside, before the rescuers, Il-Em and Yo-El nod to one another, grasp some of the particles covering themselves, and slowly part the covering. The rescuers gasp and call out, some trembling, others falling to the ground, their bodies heaving, as they *remember*.

The Light of Yo-El and Il-Em is starting to leak outside the structure. Seeing this, great numbers of brothers and sisters come rushing towards it, led by the silently provoking massmind-thing. They are yelling, cursing, attempting to combat the Light, and somehow having discovered the lines of Light from those in the Intent, are pulling on them. In all this and more, they are attempting to cause the Light to not-be!

Within the structure, Yo-El speaks to the rescuers with authority. "You must choose now!" All but one shed their forms and rush to be embraced, colliding with each other in a mighty burst of Light. Yo-El moves to the remaining one. She is doing that weeping-thing. "I so very dearly love my brothers and sisters here in the Earth-Place. How can I leave them behind?"

Yo-El extends his Light to Her until She feels a memory from what seems so long ago. Remembering the Shining One and wishing to be reunited with Him, She frees Herself from Her form.

Instantly, the rescuers are rushed into the Intent and, in a flash of brilliance, to cursing from the brothers and sisters, the Intent and all within are gone, as the massmind-thing retreats, groping about for what it had nearly claimed as its own.

Beyond the No-Place, Yo-El and the others are gathered with the rescuers. God is suddenly in their midst:

"You have given all that you knew to give and have done so without violating the Law: that the will and choice is ever free.

You have also come to the Knowing that, when you seek such a work in my name, it is very, very good for you to remember that we are one. Henceforth, then, do all you do in oneness with me, not of yourselves alone." God then leaves them to their wonder.

All are gazing at each other in awe, reliving what has just transpired. They pledge their Oneness to one another and to ever bear the Truth of God's Love.

The Guardian then comes before them. "What you pledge shall be a part of what is known as the Living Promise, that wherever one calls out unto God, there shall be the answer in His name. I, as the Guardian of the Way, shall ever be with you in this."

They return Home.

The rescuers share their experience with God and with the others. And they each affirm, before God and all, the Knowing of their uniquely personal inner Light that is of such profound and unending beauty.

They Know this to such a completeness that they are now just as the Shining One: They can be wherever they choose and in whatever experience, event, or capacity, without ever leaving the Truth of who they are and the Knowing of the presence of God. These who have known the illusion of entrapment and have returned to the Truth come to be known as the *Elders,* in recognition and honor of their accomplishment. They represent this "path of return" to any who would so choose it.

~~~~~~

Three Pertinent Excerpts
From Earlier Lama Sing Works

"In those times long past your present time (indeed, hundreds of thousands of Earth years prior to the present) a soul group came upon a much larger group that was centered around the works being done by another group of souls who had entered a realm, a place of consciousness, which has since become named Earth.

"In that time so long ago, the souls in the consciousness of Earth were struggling to understand their inner power. They knew themselves to be Children of God, and they knew therefore that they had considerable power. What they did not know was how they might use this power ... if there were limits and in what ways they might express themselves as individual souls in this realm.

"All of these activities came about during that time when the Earth was in a state of change, geologically speaking. The spirit of God expressed as the force of nature was active and creating and shifting in order to balance the Earth to make it more pleasant and livable for these souls. Unbeknownst to the souls themselves, this was taking place. All they saw, you see, was the result of God's work.

"The souls in the Earth consciousness began to create

all manner of things, becoming very involved with what they were doing. They were concentrating so intensely upon their work that they gradually began to forget who they were and what their potential is. They were creating things, plants, animals, and often these things would become a focal point such that these souls would actually, in a spiritual form or in basic energy form, enter into their creations. The reason they did so was to understand what it felt like. They wanted to know how it felt to be a tree, an animal, or any other thing that they may have created. This was the second step, so to say, away from the God consciousness.

"The creations of these souls began to interact with one another on the very material level. In other words, for example, the animals began to interact with one another, with the souls within them. See? So it was actually the souls interacting with one another as animals or as their own creations.

"The greater soul group had observed all of this activity and became concerned about their brothers and sisters who were now in the Earth realm so deeply involved in it that they had forgotten who and what they were. The concern on the part of this very large soul group was that if this continued and if more and more souls went to the Earth and became involved in these activities (which seemed to some to be nothing more than a wonderful game at that time), that they would not be able to find their way back. Already they could see that some souls were acting more like the animals than themelves. A sense of competitiveness, where they tried to outdo one another to create larger and better creations began to evolve, too.

"This greater soul group was centered around several souls who were thought of as leaders, but one was thought of in the primary sense. This one was later to become called Amelius and also had, throughout time, a number of other names. Here we find that Amelius developed a plan, an approach, that would not violate God's Universal Laws (the Laws that protect the rights and choices of others) but would, *by being an example*, enable the souls now caught up in their own creation to become free."

~~~

"So it unfolded, not only on Earth but elsewhere, in this realm and that, and the concern grew. It also became apparent that, at this point, the group of observers could no longer perceive its outcome. They considered returning to the center of Consciousness, which is God. They considered all manner of potential solutions and alternatives. But they remembered, and they remembered with joy and unqualified love. That love was borne equally to each and every one of the experimenters, who were now calling upon the elements to outdo one another and devising means by which one could consume, literally, the other's creation.

"The groups of observers who had not yet entered into the firmament remembered what God had sent forth to cause creation to unfold: His Word. They knew it to be that eternal Light that would, when sought by any individual soul, be capable of guiding that soul and all souls back to their True nature. And they created their song in accordance with God's Laws, and in an act of profound love and utter grace taken from God Himself, they placed this song within the center each of their brethren, so that no depth of finiteness could be accomplished wherefrom they could not find their way back to God. That even in the utter depths of darkness, there would be this Song of Light within them."

~~~

"And so there was this very large group of souls,

within which there are many smaller groups, each of which having chosen specific unique works that they feel best suited for and which bring them the greatest joy, whose intent included to learn how to deal with the relationships between humans, that they might help one person to another and individuals to groups find joy in themselves and in one another, overlooking any shortfalls, any limitations, anything that wasn't perhaps as beautiful as the next, and to help eliminate this sense of competitiveness, this sense of trying to be better than the next and the next.

"For as each would understand themselves to be individual and that God had created them to be Unique, that this Uniqueness was a joy to God, and that efforts to be something other than self would be, in essence, going against God's perfect plan. This work on the part of these souls was and is a very valuable contribution to the greater soul group, a group which might be well called the Sons and Daughters of the Law of One. See?"

~~~

"As you see your own Light growing and look about you and see the appearance of darkness also growing and habits of old being re-ignited, do not dwell in this, for know yours to be the greater opportunity and theirs to be the last vestiges of antiquity.

"The Earth and those spheres adjacent to her are now rising upon a crescent of Light in this, the Great Cycle. Those who cannot pass through the portal of Light will not endure. They will not die, they will not be destroyed. But there will be the division according to the Law as those who progress and raise their conscious levels of acceptance of their True spiritual nature shall move and dwell in joyous harmony and plenty."

-Lama Sing

Books by Al Miner & Lama Sing

The Chosen: *Backstory to the Essene Legacy*
The Promise: *Book I of The Essene Legacy*
The Awakening: *Book II of The Essene Legacy*
The Path: *Book III of The Essene Legacy*

In Realms Beyond: *Book I of The Peter Chronicles*
In Realms Beyond: *Study Guide*
Awakening Hope: *Book II of The Peter Chronicles*
Return to Earth: *Book III of The Peter Chronicles*

How to Prepare for The Journey:
       Vol I. Death, Dying, and Beyond
       Vol II. *The Sea of Faces*

Jesus: *Book I*
Jesus: *Book II*

The Course in Mastery

When Comes the Call

Seed Thoughts
Seed Thoughts to Consciousness

Stepstones: Compilation 1

The "Little Book" Series:
       The Children's Story

About Al Miner

A chance hypnosis session in 1973 began Al's tenure as the channel for Lama Sing. Since then, nearly 10,000 readings have been given in a trance state answering technical and personal questions on such topics as science, health and disease, history, geophysical, spiritual, philosophical, metaphysical, past and future times, and much more. The validity of the information has been substantiated and documented by research institutions and individuals, and those receiving personal readings continue to refer others to Al's work based on the accuracy and integrity of the information in their readings. In 1984, St. Johns University awarded Al an honorary doctoral degree in parapsychology.

Al conducts a variety of field research projects, as well as occasional workshops and lectures. He is no longer accepting requests for personal readings, but, rather, is devoting his remaining time to works intended to be good for all. Much of his current research is dedicated to the concept that the best of all guidance is that which comes from within. Al lives with his wife in Florida.

You can read more about Al's life and works at the Lama Sing website: *www.lamasing.net.*

www.ingramcontent.com/pod-product-compliance
Lightning Source LLC
Chambersburg PA
CBHW060547030426
42337CB00021B/4474